Distinctions in Nature

Migratory and Resident Birds Explained

Ruth Bjorklund

Cavendish Square

New York

Published in 2017 by Cavendish Square Publishing, LLC
243 5th Avenue, Suite 136, New York, NY 10016

Library of Congress Cataloging-in-Publication Data

Names: Bjorklund, Ruth, author.
Title: Migratory and resident birds explained / Ruth Bjorklund.
Description: New York : Cavendish Square Publishing, [2017] |
Series: Distinctions in nature | Includes bibliographical references and index.
Identifiers: LCCN 2016021850 (print) | LCCN 2016024367 (ebook) |
ISBN 9781502621696 (pbk.) | ISBN 9781502621702 (6 pack) |
ISBN 9781502621719 (library bound) | ISBN 9781502621726 (E-book)
Subjects: LCSH: Migratory birds–Juvenile literature. |
Birds–Wintering–Juvenile literature. | Adaptation (Biology)–Juvenile literature. |
Bird watching–Juvenile literature.
Classification: LCC QL698.9 .B625 2017 (print) | LCC QL698.9 (ebook) | DDC
598.156/8–dc23
LC record available at https://lccn.loc.gov/2016021850

Editorial Director: David McNamara
Editor: Fletcher Doyle
Copy Editor: Rebecca Rohan
Associate Art Director: Amy Greenan
Designer: Stephanie Flecha
Production Coordinator: Karol Szymczuk
Photo Research: J8 Media

The photographs in this book are used by permission and through the courtesy of:
Cover (left) Rich Reid/National Geographic Magazines/Getty Images; Cover (right) Ron Erwin/All Canada Photos/Getty Images; p. 4 svic/Shutterstock.com; p. 6 (left) Gary Unwin/Shutterstock.com; p. 6 (right) Jaroslav77/Shutterstock.com; p. 7 Jimmy phu Huynh/Shutterstock.com; p. 8 Paul Reeves Photography/Shutterstock.com; p. 10 Pavel Burchenko/Shutterstock.com; p. 11 (top) francesco de marco/Shutterstock.com; p. 11 (bottom) Danyu/Shutterstock.com; p. 12 StevenRussellSmithPhotos/Shutterstock.com; p. 14 AHPhotoswpg/iStock/Thinkstock; p. 15 JKlingebiel/Shutterstock.com; p. 17 valleyboi63/Shutterstock.com; p. 18 Happy Together/Shutterstock.com; p. 19 FotoRequest/Shutterstock.com; p. 20 (top) Michael G McKinne/Shutterstock.com; p. 20 (bottom) bobloblaw/iStock/Thinkstock; p. 22 (left) Lori Skelton/Shutterstock.com; p. 22 (right) FotoRequest/Shutterstock.com; p. 24 Elliotte Rusty Harold/Shutterstock.com; p. 26 (left) KellyNelson/Shutterstock.com; p. 26 (right) Imagery is/Moment Open/Getty Images; p. 27 Tony Moran/Shutterstock.com.

Printed in the United States of America

Contents

Sparrows are common but shy birds who perch on branches and hide in grasses to feed on insects, seeds, and berries.

Introduction: Taking Wing

Stroll through a park on a summer day and the trees and bushes are alive with birdcalls and the swish of flapping wings. In winter, the same walk is quite different. Many birds of summer are visitors. In areas where winters are cold, fewer birds remain.

There are about ten thousand different **species** of birds in the world. Birds possess an amazing variety of features—size, color, sounds, behaviors, and more. Yet birds share many common **characteristics**.

Feathered Friends

Birds are the only animals with feathers, although some birds are flightless. Some flightless birds are emus and penguins. Birds are **vertebrates**, meaning that they have a backbone. The bones of birds are hollow and lightweight.

Emus are flightless birds, but they have tiny wings under their feathers.

Birds' nests protect eggs and chicks from heat and cold.

Birds have a single V-shaped collarbone, commonly called a "wishbone," to protect their hearts and lungs while beating their wings. They do not have teeth, but they have a hard covering around their mouths. It is called a bill. All birds lay eggs.

Need for Food

Birds have a high **metabolism**, meaning they turn food and water into energy quickly. Some hummingbirds eat eight times their body weight a day. But no matter how like or unlike birds are from one another, they are skillful in adapting to their **environment**.

Hummingbirds feed on high-energy foods such as nectar and insects.

The American white pelican is a huge and powerful bird with a 9-foot (2.75-meter) wingspan.

18 Migratory and Resident Birds

If you look overhead on an autumn day, you may see birds on their winter **migration**. "Migration" comes from a Latin word meaning "to change." When animals migrate, they move from one region to another. Birds migrate to breed, grow, find better food sources, and to escape cold weather.

Migratory Birds

In the northern parts of North America, such as Canada, Alaska, and New England,

Swallows capture insects and return to their nests to feed their young.

many migratory birds, such as swallows, warblers, and flycatchers, spend the long daylight hours of summer feasting on plentiful insects, worms, and caterpillars. But as the days grow short and the weather cools, migratory birds take flight for warmer climates. Many migratory birds fly between Alaska and Mexico twice a year.

Resident Birds

Resident birds remain in the same region year round. Some North American birds are resident in one region

Zoom In

Arctic terns make the longest migration. Their trip from nesting grounds in the Arctic Circle to Antarctica is more than 25,000 miles (40,000 km).

The cardinal is a year-round resident in many US states.

but not another, but many regions share familiar species. Ravens and crows spend the winter in many areas of the **continent**. Pigeons and doves make year-round homes in both city and country. Finches, chickadees, jays, and some birds of prey such as eagles also brave cold winters.

Resident chickadees forage for insects, seeds, and fruit, and sometimes store food to eat later.

2 Comparing Migratory and Resident Birds

Migratory and resident birds use different means to survive. The main difference between them is where they make their homes.

Migratory Birds

Most birds seek warm places to build their nests, lay their eggs, and feed and raise their young. During long summer days, thousands of species of insects hatch, providing a rich food supply. Migratory birds slurp flying

In the summer, robins can eat up to fourteen earthworms a day.

insects out of the air or peck for bugs in trees. They also feast on worms and caterpillars.

But when the weather cools and the insects are gone, migratory birds leave for warmer climates. There are three types of migratory birds. In North America, many fly to Alaska and Canada in the spring, where they nest, fatten up, and raise their young. They go south for winter.

Sandhill cranes migrate in flocks of tens of thousands and fly very high.

Another type lives spring through autumn in a moderate climate, such as southern Canada and the northern United States. In winter, they make a short migration to states such as Florida or Texas. Some migrate from mountains to lowlands, such as the mountain chickadee.

Transient migratory birds, such as sandhill cranes, nest in the far north and spend the winter in Mexico or Central or South America. They fly over Canada and the United States and make brief stopovers to feed and build strength for the rest of their journey. Migratory birds follow the same pathways, or **flyways**, every year. There are four major flyways in North America—Pacific, Atlantic, Central, and Mississippi.

Resident Birds

Resident birds do not endure difficult journeys, but they face other problems. Resident birds have adapted to living in harsh environments and are resourceful at finding food and staying warm.

One of the most common resident birds is the pigeon. It can nest in scrub brush and on window ledges. It lives on seeds, berries, insects, and whatever else it can find. Many live in cities and take advantage of food left by humans. Finches are also comfortable living near humans.

Quiet winter mornings are often disrupted by the caws of ravens and crows. These black birds are clever at finding food and are **territorial** in protecting food sources. They raid other birds' nests and eat almost anything—seeds, grains, eggs, worms, and baby birds. They hide food in the grass, in trees, or behind rocks.

Goldfinches often rely on food in feeders during the winter.

Zoom In

Some birds migrate in daylight and some at night, to avoid predators. They navigate using stars, the sun, wind, landforms, and Earth's magnetic field.

Some resident birds, such as nuthatches, eat a lot in September to store fat for winter. During the coldest days, they peck at snow or ice for water. Many grow additional feathers for warmth and make their nests warm by using twigs, bark, fur, and hair. They often perch together to stay warm.

Resident birds are more territorial than migratory birds. Most eat seeds and grains and have short sharp bills to crack open shells. Resident birds tend to weigh more. Migratory birds, with their slim bills, eat insects, worms, and caterpillars. They are stronger than resident birds.

The nuthatch eats insects and seeds, and feeds upside down.

1. Baltimore orioles are a frequent sight in fruit orchards.

2. A ruffed grouse waits for spring to begin his mating dance.

3 Be a Bird Detective

1. In May, North Americans begin seeing colorful Baltimore orioles feast on insects, fruit, and nectar. In autumn, there are few insects and most fruit trees and bushes are bare. Is the oriole a migratory or a resident bird?

2. The ruffed grouse has short wings and a stubby bill. It feeds on seeds and burrows in snow caves to stay warm. Is it a resident or a migratory bird? Give some reasons.

3. Snowy egrets nest in groups in wetlands and on protected islands.

4. Pileated woodpeckers are very loud and very large, and they live in forests.

3. In early spring, flocks of snowy egrets arrive along the northern coastlines to build their nests. Are snowy egrets migratory or resident birds? Why?

4. A loud knocking in the forest in January is followed by a glimpse of red. A red-headed pileated woodpecker

is feeding on bugs and seeds buried in tree bark. Is the pileated woodpecker a migratory or resident bird, and why?

Answer Key:

1. Baltimore orioles are migratory. When their food sources disappear, they leave to find fruit and more insects to eat.

2. The ruffed grouse is a resident bird. Resident birds eat mostly seeds and grains. They have short wings and are unable to fly far. They can survive in cold weather.

3. Snowy egrets are migratory birds. They migrate to northern areas in spring to build nests.

4. Pileated woodpeckers are resident birds and survive winter by hunting for food in tree bark.

Only a few northern mockingbirds migrate, usually the ones living in high altitudes or very cold climates.

4 Rule Breakers

Some resident and migratory birds behave in unexpected ways. For example, some migratory birds stop migrating; instead, they become resident birds in warm climates, such as northern mockingbirds in Texas.

Tough Travelers

Most resident birds build nests early, before migratory birds arrive. But resident American goldfinches wait until late summer. Resident birds are usually more territorial than migratory birds. But migratory hummingbirds guard their territory ferociously.

Hummingbirds are so territorial they will fight their offspring once they have left the nest.

Bar-headed geese often fly at night and never stop flapping their wings while flying.

Most birds migrate at less than 2,000 feet (610 m), but bar-headed geese migrate from India to Mongolia over the Himalayas, the tallest mountains in the world. The geese reach altitudes of more than 21,000 feet (6,400 m).

Staying Home

Canada geese migrate between the far north and Mexico along all four North American flyways. But once they were hunted nearly to **extinction**, so officials

Canada geese can be found nearly everywhere—beaches, lakesides, riverbanks, parks, farm fields, and backyards.

bred Canada geese in **captivity**. Those geese and their offspring never learned how to migrate. Today, across the United States, many Canada geese thrive as resident birds.

captivity The condition of being raised and cared for by humans in a controlled environment.

characteristics Typical features or qualities that belong to a person, species, place, or thing that help identify it.

continent One of the large divisions of land on Earth, such as Antarctica or North America.

environment The conditions such as weather in an area in which something lives.

extinction The condition of being gone from the world forever.

flyway A flight path followed by migratory birds.

magnetic field An area affected by magnetic forces. The North and South Poles have the strongest magnetic fields on Earth.

metabolism The chemical processes by which a living thing uses food and water to grow and make energy.

migration The act of moving from one region to another.

navigate To find a way when traveling to get to a specific place.

resident Living in one place for some length of time.

species A scientific class of plants or animals that are similar and can reproduce.

territorial The act of occupying and defending a chosen area.

transient Staying only a short period of time before moving on.

vertebrates A large group of animals, including humans, which have a backbone made of bone or cartilage.

Find Out More

Books

Burnie, David. *Bird-Watcher*. New York: DK Publishing, 2015.

Cate, Annette. *Look Up! Bird-Watching in Your Own Backyard*. Somerville, MA: Candlewick Press, 2013.

Catt, Thessaly. *Migrating with the Arctic Tern*. New York: PowerKids Press, 2011.

Websites

Smithsonian Migratory Bird Center: Fact Sheets
http://nationalzoo.si.edu/scbi/migratorybirds/fact_sheets
This website links to fact sheets about migratory birds, their characteristics, and their journeys.

US Fish and Wildlife Service: Bird Enthusiasts
https://www.fws.gov/birds/index.php
This government agency posts links to news about birds and bird conservation groups.

Index

Page numbers in **boldface** are illustrations.

Ruth Bjorklund loves to watch birds. From her home on Bainbridge Island, near Seattle, Washington, she can see great blue herons, bald eagles, chickadees, ravens, and more. She has written numerous books for young people on a wide range of subjects, including wild parrots and wildlife rescue.